Our Cities Vanish

Our Cities Vanish

Ray Hinman

edited by Tim Wood

Dallas   Colorado Springs   GrandViaduct.com

Our Cities Vanish
Published by GrandViaduct
www.GrandViaduct.com

Copyright © 2009 GrandViaduct
Poems Copyright © 2009 Ray Hinman
Cover Image Copyright © 2009 Kelvin Burr

Cover image by Kelvin Burr (www.kelvinburrart.com)
Design and Typesetting by BuzzGlass (www.buzzglasss.com)

The following poems were previously published:
The New World Order #1, Corporations Buy and Sell, Whitman's
Ghost Takes a Tour of the City, Border Town, Beauty in the Brain
and Archives were published in *Negations: An Interdisciplin-
ary Journal of Social Criticism* (Volume 1, Issue 2); Hobos Near
Tacoma, Our Cities Will Vanish, After Reading Marcuse, Double
Entry, And Then He Sold the Third World, The Thing You Will Miss
Most were published in *Negations: An Interdisciplinary Journal
of Social Criticism* (Vol 1, Issue 1); Our Cities Will Vanish in *the
Word: the monthly Guide to the Arts in Dallas*, April 1997.

First Edition, Original Release

Library of Congress Cataloging-in-Publication Data applied for -
available via publisher's website when obtained

ISBN-10: 0-9824087-0-6
ISBN-13: 978-0-9824087-0-4

Dedicated to my parents A.D. and Virginia Hinman, Joe,
Lance, Patty, Jim, Rowdy, Arnie, George McGovern and
Herbert Marcuse.

Contents

The Poetry of Ray Hinman
Genealogy, Craft and Shamanistic Creation

by Tim Wood

The curse of many freshman poetry classes is that they are an extended explication of dictionary definitions of poetry and related words. A dictionary is useful for characterizing things that are finite, literal, quantifiable. But, like many technical tools, they have limits which exist somewhere short of poetry and God.

Poetry does not have the pretension of exploring literal truth, and it isn't a thing, as a whole, that you can hold in your hand. With Ray Hinman's poetry, a good starting point is the idea of the Hero and the heroic journey in Fraer and later Campbell. The Hero leaves the known world, goes somewhere else —often strange and unusual— makes a discovery and returns to share it with his people.

Art can be an heroic act. The privilege of being an outsider is that the journey can occur while sitting at an iHop and wondering about the people at the next table. *Why is a black couple sitting down and laughing with two people who have all the visual marks of being skinheads?* The journey is heroic because it takes one beyond the world that is normally known.

Such heroic journeys exist throughout Ray Hinman's poetry. "The Ex-Missionary Learns Mexico" begins:

> After the rain we came into the low
> country, the hills unrolled beneath us,
> pitted with arroyos; green aloe vera plants,
> concealed basins where water stood,

hidden from high ground like secret lakes.
We climbed from our horses and looked into
a pond, our faces shining against sky
and cloud.

In the first stanza, we have the entire heroic journey: leaving the known, the discovery, the telling. And, we also run smack into that which is secret, hidden, mysterious.

Ray Hinman's poetry can be like journeying across the desert to a secret well and returning with the water. You can see that concretized in this poem. The water at the well is rain, the things pulled from the well are both visual —*hills unrolled, concealed basins*— and the hidden, the mysterious —*hidden from high ground like secret lakes.*

Stepping back, a poem is a journey the poet takes us on via words. The same is true of all verbal art forms whether fiction, movie scripts or poetry. With fiction and movie scripts, terminology like plot and character development are ways of discussing different types of journey within the work of art.

But, there is a type of impatience about most poetry that demands that the poet strip the superfluous such as plot that lengthens the journey. "A Philosopher is Born in the Tropics" opens with an establishing shot: we see the ex-missionary again. He's in a cafe filled with people. He's "aloof" from them, separated. He's sitting with a glass of wine. The rest of the poem is the discovery:

He steeps in his own lush thought—
puffs of color fed by moss, by the death
and rebirth of the moon and sun,
nourished but steeping to a wilted lump.

The bond between love and beauty double:

A ghost walks through my skull, my image-laden skull.

from *Images from a Relationship,* p. 103

droning waves, speculations, the wheel
that takes the sun and stars around... love traces
it among the skies; God drawn by dots.

But to trace their beauty out in jungle
is to leave the blossom halted, half formed.
Beauty of heaven or a woman's body, either side
of love is the patch of light floating in wine.

What we hear is truth captured in a moment of inner
experience, not the story of a great battle won. The Ex-
Missionary has transcended religion with a vision of death
and rebirth, the progression of the stars, the limits of mortal
portraits of God, the limits of tracing any of this in the
jungle. And, by extension, the limits of portraying what he
has learned in images or, tragically, words.

A Genealogy of Poetry

Understanding where something comes from gives it a
kind of meaning. People study their own genealogy.
The Bible has the descendents of Adam and the genealogies
of Jesus. Poetry has a genealogy, too. It's fairly easy to draw
the line of poetry back through say the bards then Homer
and reach the first storytellers telling stories around the fire.
I think Ray Hinman would argue otherwise. Pulling pieces
from "The Shaman Considers His Craft":

But then I got to naming things,
and relating one thing to another....

I had to know that beauty—decode it,
like a song....

I had to know what made the haunted real,
to know how these doors open...

And at that point, that beauty ... became
so brittle...
I missed the whole haunted meaning of fire
and magic both.
And I was left there, as if I stood before
a maze of bushes all grown with doors.

The poem tells us that naming, decoding, explaining strips
away the beauty, removes the mystery and leaves you
trapped.

A fundamental part of storytelling and fiction is naming
things —protagonist and antagonist— and relating them
via plot and character development. In most successful fic-
tion the relating is done via conflict. The obsession is not
with truth but with conflict, development and resolution.

Most poets avoid storytelling techniques for pragmatic
reasons: they usually aren't necessary to poetry. Character
development and plot are only used if absolutely necessary.
But, here, Hinman is explicitly disavowing storytelling as
the basis of poetry on a philosophical level: what makes sto-
rytelling *storytelling* undermines the fundamental purpose
of poetry.

Schweitzer notes that we divide the arts according to the
materials used with "one who employs colors, a painter;
one who uses words, a poet. This, however, is a purely
external division. In reality, the material which the artist
expresses himself is a secondary matter.....Various artists
have their habitation in his soul....and they always choose
the language that best suits them best." (*J. S. Bach, Volume
Two*, p. 8).

I'm curious whether Hinman would argue that Homer
isn't poetry. It is clearly grand storytelling and is chock full

of poetic techniques. Just as clearly, many have pointed out that rhyme and meter were not developed so we could have poetry. They were developed as memorization aids: if I get to a line and a forget a word or two, the fact that the line has to follow the rhythmic structure of the poem and end with "sounds like" eases the burden on the storyteller.

I'm certain that the fact that I just accused Homer of not being a Poet has elicited screams from poetry experts who believe poetry can be defined by what techniques it uses and who, I believe, are guilty of (to use the now worn vernacular) not "getting it".

But, if poetry is not storytelling, what is it? What are the roots of poetry? Hinman provides partial answers to both questions in the title of this poem: "The Shaman Considers his Craft". The Poet, like the Priest, is a descendant of the Shaman. Poetry is a Craft.

Postmodernism was clearly bent (arguably centrally bent) on the demolition of all sorts of things including artificial constructions like "High Art" and (low) craft. But, the Shaman's Craft is not the craft that postmodernism tried to elevate. It is a different meaning of the word.

Some people say art is self expression. That's like saying that whining about why you don't own a Porsche is art. Having something to "express" does not make one a poet anymore than having a tube of paint to squeeze until it pops makes one a painter or a dermatologist.

The difference is something acquired through learning and practice: the Craft of poetry (or the craft of painting or the craft of songwriting). Acquiring mechanical skills (ability to type, how to use a dictionary, knowledge of different techiques) is a necessary part of becoming a craftsman but it is just an element. Another element is developing a feel for the material, a sense of when to use one technique versus another.

Perhaps more importantly, craftsmanship involves knowing when the rules are getting in the way of what you are trying to achieve. With poetry, we saw this with the abandonment of Rhyme and Meter as a requirement. Rhyme and Meter are useful tools but if they interfere with Crafting the poem, why use them?

The Shamanistic in Poetry

Claiming a descent from the Shaman certainly seems somewhat counter-intuitive. *Who would want to claim descent from primitive guys painted up to deceive even more primitive guys?*

It's better to think of the Shaman (at least in this context) as someone who exists to connect people with the transcendent and the sublime. Other people exist to handle the needs of survival: creating order, providing food, etc.

But, what is the point of an existence that is just survival? Shamans exist to provide an answer to that question and to be a conduit to the answer. In "Muses, Madonnas and Modernity", an interplay between Craft and the poetic Shaman flows through the poem:

> whoever carved the St. Demetra of Eleusis
> thought he knew a woman who could contain
> the cosmos...
>
> Ardor burns the glazed muse into modernity,
> but the dome of the church will not open
> or crack, those realms where images reign always
> descend, gazing on the rough-hewn wood will not
> carry us far once we leave the vestry;

...I hope against feeble reality for a Madonna
of desire, but if you hope your gaze is rewarded
by her grace, then a glance is all you get.

The Greek Muse of Poetry inspired the poet. Even today,
poets talk about the Muse because for many poets, the
poem —or at least the epiphany that initiates it— seems to
come from nowhere. The poet's purpose (and usually obses-
sion) is to use Craft to execute that vision.

"The Shaman Considers His Craft" ends with the poet
trapped:

> And at that point, that beauty ... became
> so brittle...
> I missed the whole haunted meaning of fire
> and magic both.
> And I was left there, as if I stood before
> a maze of bushes all grown with doors.

Inspiration has been obscured in the need to name, relate
and characterize rather than to be a poet. And that failure
has left him in "a maze of bushes all grown with doors". It
reminds me of Elmer Fudd chasing Bugs Bunny around
a hallway as doors breed like rabbits. It also reminds me
of a darker version of Alice in Wonderland or many of
Magritte's paintings. It's a place full of doors that lead no-
where with the meaning —of fire and magic both— missed,
lost.

If you also trace Priests and Preachers back to Shamans,
then the divergence between Poets on one hand and Priests
and Preachers on the other, was in a moment that Hin-
man describes here. One version of this idea is expressed in
thoughts like "I'm spiritual but not religious". In that phras-

Tim, the adman,
rises to murder his
wife, or her cat, or
perhaps a random
variable... he ascends
the ladder into a
neon bliss.

from *Suburban Prophet,* p. 110

ing, religion is the practice of mapping the maze, describing the doors and delineating the rules on the use of each door. The focus becomes moral message and the practice is one of sermonizing. The result is people fleeing the Church because they sense that God isn't in the House.

Gnosticism

A diverse range of movements in early Christianity (termed heretical by the Orthodox churches) termed Gnosticism believed in two ideas that are relevant here. First, people are divine souls trapped in the material world. Second, the concept of gnōsis: there is a hidden, esoteric knowledge that can be revealed and reminds the spiritual in people of their true origins. Revealing this knowledge is a way to free people and reconnect them to the divine. In the poem "Gnostic":

> St. Peter drew a bubble burst
> by a saint with a bulging eye.
> Walls of stone and the pagan priestess
> prepare the leg of hollow-eyed
>   beggars.
> Still the vision lay beyond his raptured
> senses,
>   and no sight returned
> as Hosanna rose with fragrant incense;
>   the world lay ready for his fiery word.
> From the mountains came rejoicing...
>
> He droned against it...
>
> We drove the camels, chest high in swirling dust,
>   laying waste to the snares and tares of hell.
> Then a holy terror seized us, and the world

was woven into a tapestry of dust.

Gnosticism echoes Kabbalah and its focus on hidden, eso-
teric knowledge about (among other things) a Creator —
eternal, infinite and essentially unknowable— and methods
of learning aimed at spiritual realization.

In this sense, both Gnosticism and Kabbalah have deeply
Shamanistic echoes. The Shaman is the conduit to the
hidden, fundamentally unknowable, divine. He struggles
with communicating something rationally unknowable and
infinite with those who spend their time obsessed with the
shallowness of the surface. In "When I Enter the King-
dom":

> Summer burns inside us,
> its reflection shines, even if unseen, and out does
> the fire of clouds and the poison of indignation.
> But we never choose to understand it.
> It was sent to us as a consolation, while better gifts
> perished among the blazing of planets, the sighting
> of stars, the solstice that divides sight from light.
>
> Was it as if the poison of drugs
> had made us stronger, had given the season just to us?
> Proteus rising, Venus rising, Ganja scent
> rising in the night air.
> When I and I enter the kingdom our eyes will burn
> like glass... when grass and grass
> begin their blazing, a new kingdom will enter itself....

Summer doesn't literally burn inside any more than the
reflections of the sun can be hidden. Right at the beginning
of the poem, he shifts us into the realm of metaphor, the
land beyond the rational. The fact that all of this has been

lost —we never chose to understand it— indicates this is a choice we made by deciding not to choose, a passive aggressive fall where we didn't choose to not eat the apple.

But, of course, the apple is from the tree of the knowledge of good and evil. The apple is knowledge. Clearly the Shaman treads a boundary between what is forbidden and what is allowed. In ancient Judaism the Priest was the only one allowed into the Temple's Inner Sanctum. Before entering there was an elaborate purification ritual to ensure that he was Holy lest he be struck down by God. And, just in case there was a slip, a rope was tied around his waist so the body could be pulled out in the case of failure.

Life, Death, Rebirth

Hinman had an occult streak. He dabbled in ceremonial magic and studied Kabbalah before it became a fashion statement. And, while his poetry isn't about preaching, he strives to journey and return to construct a world out of literary allusion, a world in which we can talk with the dead and return reborn. He makes this explicit in "After the Passionate Argument":

> If voices could rise from Ilios, rise
> from the ground, speaking to this bitter age,
> to those who have rejected rain and murdered
> wind swept thickets, our mockery of ancient truth
>   could redeem us.
>
> We would see as they saw...

As some say of God, "not choosing, you still have made a choice". There is a truth that can be lost and death is the result:

Truth is lost like night air rising, its scent
pleads from fallow ground, but it's drowned out
by groans coming up from battlements.
Youth is lost in its own evolution, it retains
the mark of lightening and thunder's echo:

below the window crossvine clings, no flowers,
but a brittle, gray stalk.

But, here, death is a very different thing. It is death in a
cycle of life, death and rebirth. Returning to "A Philoso-
pher is Born in the Tropics":

He steeps in his own lush thought—
puffs of color fed by moss, by the death
and rebirth of the moon and sun...

This death and rebirth is systemic. It is a cycle not just
of life, but of the moon and stars and, presumably, the
universe itself: all the things in the created realm. In the
mythologies of Mesoamerica, time is described in terms of
cycles. The short ones are the rise and fall and rise of the
sun, the cycles of the moon and seasons. But, they believed
in larger cycles measured in thousands and hundreds of
thousands of years including the one ending in 2012 that
has caused such a buzz recently. Of course, Hinman's inter-
est predates the current obsession and isn't focused on the
distraction of a single moment in time.

In the poem "Monte Albán", even the oldest spirits have
knowledge that we can learn:

Older men go north of the Zócalo to drink;
    squatting in small groups
    outside shabby bars, they sing
very old songs and talk about their women.

This side of freedom saddens Juarez;
but the older guardians up in the hills,
   the old Zapotec spirits who
      watch over Monte Albán,
they know one generation cultivates another
   in the clarity of wind...
the old spirits are as aloof as the stones
   where they sit reigning over the region.
You have to know them to see their passion,
   you have to know them through the place.
You have to walk through the wind temple
      letting the narrow passages
take you up to the stone-carved heaven,
the heaven laid out by stars... or twirl
   into the rock with the geometric dancer,
twirl into regions that send the wind across
   fields gorged out in the sides of steep
peaks.

It is a knowledge that requires a journey outside of the dis-
tractions, a journey away from the things we use to drown
the spirit, where the spirit is the thing within that can have
conversations with the dead —whether spirits or authors.
"Monte Albán" concludes:

The Spanish once thought the old gods
lived in a higher heaven, until they rebelled
   against their maker.
That primordial war threw them from windless
   parts of heaven to their walls and altars;
they washed the blood of one victim
   with the blood of thousands.
   What the conquistador couldn't see

We drove the camels,
chest high in swirling
dust, laying waste...
then a holy terror
seized us, and the
world was woven
into a tapestry of
dust.

from *Gnostic,* p. 83

was the wheel of myth and conquest, perhaps
it was the memory of their special place,
    of laughter leaping bright as love,
that inspired the works at Monte Albán.

Hinman's world is one vibrant with the tension between
light and darkness, life and death and a cycle involving re-
birth in which corpses can blossom again. It is also a world
created with a sense of what it is not: the world screaming
with artificial light and the "Suburban Prophet":

    Tim sets the clock that is set for eternity.
    Outside Jacob's ladder descends on the front lawn,
    glowing brighter than Broadway.
    Music of Angels rings out beyond this paper,
    His life has lead up to this vision:

        a double edged axe,
        a black robed figure with the face of Tim's
        alarm clock, figures dancing in each other's arms
            (quietly, beyond the fringe of woods)...

    Tim, the adman, rises to murder his wife,
    or her cat, or perhaps a random variable... he ascends
    the ladder into a neon bliss.

It may be a brilliant world filled with neon and visions but
they are false just the same with all the vibrance of the non-
decaying undead of the landfill. It is a consuming world
that hides things with smoke and lies about what we really
need. In "And Then He Sold the Third World", there is the
adman's muse:

    Then he sold pesticides to the third world;
    babies were born without hands and feet.

And he became a little sports car;
he sped over roads that ran by the sea.

Finally, he sold arms to the third world;
grass huts went up in flame.
He became a wardrobe, a sound system,
a rain-smeared deck for the patio.
He became everything that is bought and sold,
everything that hasn't got a mind,
everything but a man.

Dimensionality

The echoes of Marcuse's *One Dimensional Man* ring
through this poetry. Given his role as Poetry Editor at
Negations, this isn't surprising. You could hear similar ele-
ments throughout the poetry published in *Negations.* Cor-
porations create needs, false needs, in us for things we don't
need. The price is paid by us, our society and the world as
whole, now and in the future. As Hinman notes in "Clint
with Tall Hair":

> ...the profusion of our products re-
> duces us all to reflections, but takes away
> the urge to reflect; we are sifted
> through the night like iron filings.

It's not just a sense of the price we are paying and will pay,
but a mourning. He fears that there are things we are losing.
In "The Thing You Will Miss Most" we hear that:

> Against the whirl of night life
>   you hold your heart
>   like some fragile glass thing
> that hums approval or hatred.

We should lament the loss of higher things.
   But when our democracy is gone,
   this will be the thing you miss most.

He creates a world, in part, as an antidote to the common
one of death and decay that is created by selling false needs
in neon. Hinman builds that world by conversing with the
dead, talking with voices from the literary past, alluding
to things that have come before. He writes with a clear,
conscious sense that poetry is a Craft. More importantly, as
a Craftsman, he understands the value of aesthetics, culture
and meaning. And he demonstrates it both by allusion
and brushstroke, and by building it into the framing and
aesthetics of the poems themselves. His job isn't to spell out
what culture is. In "Whitman's Ghost Takes a Tour of the
City":

   But you, knowing the richer reds
   and deeper blues appear briefly at dusk
   then withdraw into their own flame...
   He goes out at evening, shirt long, baggy as a coat,
   his white beard flows from the sack-like face,
   the outstretched hat-brim,
   he has made himself bewildered; where are the poets
   chanting to the multitude? The headlong, vulgar, robust
   freedoms of the crowd? Is there only you?
   Bleating out this quick-flaring image? You chant
   the gawk-shuffle, art-patter, and wonder how the plant
   ever let you in. The inferno of the city blazes
   around us; we detail its hidden lights.

Here we have an imagining of a literal journey. The poet
steps outside, wonders about the death he feels around
him. Even the poets have been reduced from chanting to

the crowds to "gawk-shuffle, art-patter": the dilettante's
dabbling meaningless self-expression in an age where even
dilettantism has come to be viewed as not just self-obsessive
but quaint and irrelevant. This view of irrelevance is one
that poetry as a whole inflicted on itself as, for much of
the twentieth century, it became obsessed with poetry as a
written artifact rather than one that was also meant to be
spoken, chanted. But, poetry is, in its roots, a spoken —
verbal— art form. You can see this in the fact that many
think of (on one hand) Bob Dylan's writing and (on the
other) rap as poetry.

Hinman's poems are meant to be spoken, chanted, per-
haps screamed. In some poems ("Gnostic" and "Woman
of Cloth" for instance), you'll see a structure like a movie
script. Even though his references can veer to the obscure,
he chooses words no more complicated (or high falutin')
than is necessary to draw his point. For the sake of simplic-
ity, he also avoids complicated structures like rhyme and
meter. But, he will use metrical patterns. When I was in the
performance poetry ensemble "Question Authority, the",
we staged Alan Ginsburg's "Hum Bomb!" as a cross be-
tween a call and response chant, and a march. When I read
"Archives", I can hear the same effect:

> The feet
> are marching
> as waves crash.
> The feet
> are marching
> as waves crash.
> The feet
> are marching
> as the sea of fists clench.

31

The answer
is not
in the archives.
The mouths
are marching,
the mouths
are marching,
and the minds are tossing slogans
while the Elders
dream
of rivers,
and lakes,
and ladies
in flowing gowns.

At the end, the militaristic overtones collapse beneath the dreams of the Elders. It's a beautiful contrast.

Hitchhiking

Ray Hinman hitchhiked extensively when he was younger. His journeys took him up the east coast to Toronto and up the west coast to Vancouver. He talks about having a run in with a ghost at a Rescue Mission in Denver.

And, at one point, he was listening Joan Baez as she was preparing for a concert at the Hollywood Bowl. She actually tried to keep the staff from throwing him out. Perhaps because a Joan Baez would understand him more than they would.

After all, art is art. Picasso crafted in paint, Baez crafts in music, Hinman crafts in poetry. But, no matter what medium, art is still art. It is that which strives Shamanistically to tell the hero's discovery, the transcendent, the sublime.

Town emerging
ghost-like from the
desert, disappearing
like the shifting
faces. But your face
shone above it all,
barely visible but
shining, whispering
something I could
not understand.

from *Your Eyes Full of Weekends*, p. 78

Our Cities Vanish

I

Sifted Through the Night

After the Passionate Argument

Will progress bring a permanent winter?
Whole ages can unbuckle with a simple curse.

If voices could rise from Ilios, rise
from the ground, speaking to this bitter age,
to those who have rejected rain and murdered
wind swept thickets, our mockery of ancient truth
    could redeem us.

We would see as they saw, before the futile
maiden cried at dear turrets, cried things
that could have kept the world from breaking;
night left few pieces of their tale intact.

Agamemnon's boast, the choice of Paris, Helen
turned from vision to siren to visionary desire.

Truth is lost like night air rising, its scent
pleads from fallow ground, but it's drowned out
by groans coming up from battlements.
Youth is lost in its own evolution, it retains
the mark of lightening and thunder's echo:

below the window crossvine clings, no flowers,
but a brittle, gray stalk.

A Kind of Vanity

The suburban cop glares across the void
of this public room, so sure he's found a suspect.
He never quits smiling, makes sure I don't see
him look; this explains so many anonymous crimes,
the presence of this somnambulistic stranger.
He does a rude addition: my hair, with its odd,
disheveled originality, its betrayal of vanity
that refused to die with adolescence, the notebook
that contains a reality making this one pale,
my glassy eyes, my ratty clothes, the entire
aura about me: I'm soiled by a third night odor
of unclad sleep.

Mental illness is what erodes democracy.
The glaze my eyes take on in inspiration is far more
alien than his; I am a traffic light that adds:
think first, before it says go, the one set of headlights
coming up the freeway, somehow wishing it could signal
a refusal to shine like all the others,
a window that wishes it could reflect the future
as well as each present image.
The cop sits for a long time; he finds rules in addition
he's never heard of before, decides to ask the waitress
if I come in often, leaves. But he's sure some night
the window will shine the future, sure it will reveal
all the crimes yet to be committed.

Brickyard Lady

The brickyard lady has worked so long
she brings the dyepress dust home
to make brick biscuits.
If she were just a housewife, the clatter
her men make nailing up eaves
and phony sprucewood shutters would be
her coronation.

Reigning in her kitchen, reigning
over evenings strung with cowhide banners, her men
would seal her off from intrusions; only light,
and the billowing, shear drapes, and tin pans
hand-deep in flour would seep into mornings
with her men. They eat tilehard bread and snicker
when she cackles.

But her time has been allotted, fealty
owed to the warpwitted unwinding of machines, the
whompwhomping of devices
producing whatever entices... tiles
for her men to lay out the bathroom with.

At lunch she watches the wetbacks, sleek girls
with thin bodies and shining black cat-eyes.
She listens to their counterpoint, a staccato
of nasal tones that take her to the desert,
to adobe walls baking among bushy, bright green

41

Maguey; but the dyepresses always hammer again,
always thud her back to convention.
Back to blue-white rooms that flicker,
back to differentials, ball joints,
to hang-dog wisdom spilling through yellow teeth.
She reigns over everything that goes whompwhomp
in America, elbow deep in porcelain dust
making brick biscuits for her men.

While at the Economic Summit in '83 Reagan's Daughter Got Engaged to a Guru

Roses fell where the Pershings sit.
There were disheveled maidens from Megog crying:
history is grim as the sea is deep.

They conceived a house of shame,
Those born for dullness, yes, you chip through
layers or conquest when you read
　　At Bhagavad Gītā.

Apollo and Daphne, Achilles and Andromache,
Teiresias blind as the American people,
the stone house cowers at Agamemnon's boast,
the Indo-Europeans wander this way and that,
but Odysseus' bow still can't be bent.

Now you can lounge with Lamas
and offbeat Gurus, dragging the women of England
by the tails like dead priestesses; one more summit
we'll chat the mellow bric-a-brac of Zen... no need
for a last look at Britain, the Aryans
are coming home.

43

I Do Have a Job but...

am I ready now?
Goods don't care for me at all;
the blonde with the beehive hairdo
and big bosom gives a wondering look.
But her eyes are too much like mine.
Too much puzzlement, too much fear
begging to be exploited. I like the Arab
too, she flirts like a young mare.

    But Goods don't care for me.
Money never did. and I know ole Venus doesn't
like me.
Pants ragged, shirt too loose, I laugh
bad politics through broken teeth
and mutter about mythology.

The old men at the counter guzzle coffee
and laugh... a flock of old falcons gone crowing
after stale corn. It rots among sugar
spilled like sand, silver pots of bad cream.
On her next round the beehive lady
will brush my sleeve, laugh like loose silver.
She pauses to stare out over the freeway
where the morning star will rise.

Eileen Loses Her Faith

The time of indifference is over;
eyes turn from a translucent sky
to the reality of graphs and sutures.
Those lips are whiter
than your lab coat
and you wonder if you'll ever
hear them bestow another kind remark.

From the parking garage
a lone egret glides across a brittle sky,
it's grace rebukes your notion of chance,
but as it takes to the drooping tree
you add the consolations
of a new freedom:
hot dance tunes, mysterious encounters,
athletic young men with revved up cars;
can you count the little dart hurls
as you help stitch fragments of organs
and fragments of lives?
The bird suddenly falls like a tear drop;
gravity has won at last.

Pan's Wife

The house: a stone barn
with back walls that suffocate
as they protect, though the silence
indicates how safe the night really is.
The Characters: alone again, behind
white walls that shine in sun
but seem muted in darkness,
sepulcher white.
The room is full of books with immaculate
bindings, music equipment, rare
furniture, a TV set that flickers
like a small window.
The lighting is set by a finger's whim;
a stone god in the garden pipes
to revels that have never been.

An antiseptic scene, but look closer…
the woman's eyes are puffed with fine
crow's feet, her chin is no longer virginal,
merely sagging.
The friend beside her once called her
The Gertrude Stein of Dallas
(but she looked like Helen of Troy).
Now it is only in the family album that her eyes
shine from inspiration. They look medicated,
as if she had just returned from a place

where sadness is like rebirth.
She once gave up conventional beauty
for the kind that approaches terror.
But she has returned from the seduction
of innocence somehow no less innocent
than when she left.
Look even closer: the photo
     of her graduation...
draped in a flowing Gainsborough dress,
lace ruffles revealing abundant cleavage,
her hat brim is wide, tilted back
like a crown of light. Back then
her eyes were as bright as the sun on pale
sand, she could have been Pan's wife.
Such beauty could only invite destruction.
An Agamemnon of a father presided
over her childhood (until he was cuckolded
by his wife's capability).
Her destruction came
at the hands of the Taurians: gawky
young men with silly names.
Her gift was for destruction, she was
a tragic poem to herself.

But now she has returned from
pornographic evenings, the rites
of dissipation, rites that somehow never
touched her core.

She laughs easily, gives
her attention to anything, she could
even forget her own existence
if her friend would reach over and fondle
her (going giddy as she does with secret
pleasure when her own breasts bounce)
but her friend is busy summing
up the past.

She waits, clean again,
scrubbed pink and no longer at odds
with the stillness of the house.
She waits, not to ignore
his litany of problems, or his vision
of that place where the sky is pale,
the sun driven by a god, where words are more
timeless than television;
she waits for something she doesn't
know about, for leaf shadows on white walls
to recall the thread that separates pleasure
    and diligence. And we can move on,
she needs no help waiting for the night
to become so still she finds a part
of herself she never knew lay rooted like
this tree in mossy ground, or for her own
beauty to settle like a tired Oracle.

Does it Always End Like This?

Does it always end like this?
Young women drug to maternity,
moving to the city where opportunity is.
Twelve winters, summers, springs, etc.
The archetypal number of change,
    springing all seasons to their end,
and here she is again. The symbolic cycle
has seen Nixon uprooted but then every descent
value booted when the movement played out.

She still wears her hair loose,
fluffy woolen sweater, she still carries
Latin America in her looks,
though a child rides her arms incessantly.
Fresh from college,
she packed her diploma away like dowry,
readying for the day her lawyer's pools
and cars will be half hers, readying to swell
    into matronhood, a great,
bloated sack of indignant wit with a snotty voice.

All over America people wait for their wave
of conquest, passionate about a morality
they hardly understand, a love of freedom defined
by fetters.

Air and light, the sun and the night, just as
the desert and the beach draw different parts
of us to celebrate their beauties,
they play in different ways upon our weakness,
Club Med can clear the beach, scrape away the old
shanties, dwindling oil supply mushroom adobe
huts into corrugated tin cities overnight.

High on a sacrament of sugar and glutamate,
she enters the cafe's doorway,
prize student in Latin-American studies, now
lusting after the death of her subjects.
All this passes quickly, like a desert squall;
lost in its own reflection she would say.
    Her sunglasses still tilt back
over her hair, her head rides slender shoulders
like a lily pad with a long stalk.
She squints her eyes in knowing amusement:
the image of a resurgent race.

After Reading Marcuse

Alienated from work, we are alienated from the elements:
the wind flings its idiot-rattle
and binds me to its blade.
Drops stare into the oblivion of dispersal,
fire abdicates the rage of its touch.
I wander among the tables with their fine little cups;
all who drink stare dumbly,
eyes wide with no content.
Only the earth is faithful.
It holds the sediment of ages
and waits for my contribution.

And Then He Sold the Third World

First he sold tobacco to the third world,
and the cancer wards were clogged
with bloody sputum.
And he became a house filled with fine glassware,
and he shined with yellow windows
against the blue of night.

Then he sold pesticides to the third world;
babies were born without hands and feet.
And he became a little sports car;
he sped over roads that ran by the sea.

Finally, he sold arms to the third world;
grass huts went up in flame.
He became a wardrobe, a sound system,
a rain-smeared deck for the patio.
He became everything that is bought and sold,
everything that hasn't got a mind,
everything but a man.

Clint with Tall Hair

The profusion of our products reduces us
to reflections.
All men are Clint Eastwood,
    all women are shades of the same starlet.
Clint with tall hair and a raspy voice.
Clint, calling squadrons of planes to bomb
the children of Managua, or
swinging proletarian boogie through
doldrums of the crumbling wall.
Wanting to make it with the 7-Eleven girl
on his way home from work,
or stuff some haughty bitch in the ground
for a lay the whole sex denied him.
Clint Reagan, Clint Fallwell,
Clint the little "Rotcy" boy who built
a new computer.

    Yes, the profusion of our products re-
duces us all to reflections, but takes away
the urge to reflect; we are sifted
through the night like iron filings.

Solitude's Counterfeit

The roar of the freeway fades.
Here and there
a light among the rows of identical houses.
Here and there
patches of blue-gray light, framed by
a yellow window.
At this time of night I can't help thinking
how silly Rilke would look, standing on
a bridge in Farmers Branch.

Or he would look sinister.
The ornate cityscapes, the ones he loved,
knew centuries of war and upheaval; for him
they created the deepest solitude.
Buddha of the book stalls (his features proclaimed),
an orphan of art, brooding on park benches.
A dancer, though always serenely still.

Here bridges are built for speed,
the streets have no sidewalks, the creek
is only knee-deep.
Here the man who would truly go into himself
has no place to go.
And when it's really late, only the sky

is active, filled with lights
taking people off to buy bits of the cities
Rilke loved.

Embers of Sunlight

The other night I stood where we had built
    a fire on the lake shore,
remembering how the smoke rose, and floated
       among the trees.
    It was summer then—we were much younger—
    and had just met.
    Your hair was redder than dark red honey.
    The way it gleamed in the sun
made you a part of all I'd loved in books
    and in the beauty of art.
      Now I wonder,
    why is death so much more substantial
      than the things we love?

I ask that part of you left in these trees:
    somber, silent, laden with snow.
       Their branches are so empty,
        so bleak.
Within this perception, there lies
    some margin of comfort.
(We all know loved ones live on in grief)
    But for an instant it seemed
there might be some quality of grief
    that engenders joy.

But I knew each single particle
 of slush and ice
mocked and refused to let me go.

Reflection: Early Autumn

It rains:
reds and greens are growing older,
darker than the season's face.
The houses of this region grow
from a semblance of freedom, but their
streets are vague, all tended
by a mild woman whose eyes shine
like glass.

It rains:
early Autumn draws you to yourself.
Streaks of light on slick pavement,
the backyard walled in defiance
of desire.
That slow stepping woman could be anywhere,
approaching to renounce what the mood
of the day requires, to name everything
that is not an extension of you and praise
things you have no desire to own.

The Wisdom of Robinson Jeffers

Jeffers built a tower on this continent's
　　sandy warf,
and wrote of freedom as if it were a bitter drink.
The sun lay in the dregs of his cup—but not hot,
not blinding—flattened out to muted tones,
　　as if the earth's beauty
brought too much sorrow to let its fire blaze
for long. He thought Point Carmel held the dregs
of Eden, not because of its radiance, but because
　　there he was reminded
of what our father's lies really meant: this Republic
lives only in newsprint; in nature freedom is
subjected to the pathos of maggots and lice.

　　The sun cracks stone,
rivers eat their way through land;
progress is strife, not knowledge; for all the eons
it took this continent to form, the earth's plates
to shift into mountains, are only an inkling
of what it takes Democracy to make free men.
　　Yes, the eons
have improved the animal, have endowed him with
insight and ambition, but nature has not improved
the awkward dance of conquest; atoms split
into bright whirlwinds will be even more indecent
than flesh picked clean, exposed to sun.

We still watch the hawks circle
above the sea, and time has not tamed our envy.

Cross Currents

Sometimes a tress of hair, or just a scent,
can release desires that lead a life
to shards—or with luck—can put a life
back in order. A shapely leg filling out
dark stockings, a pair of breasts not quite
concealed; perhaps a single object,
a conversation piece, can trigger destiny
or throw events off course.

A piece of blossom drew us together,
but it has floated off somewhere, some region
beyond probabilities where petals go
when they float too long in streams. It holds
our probabilities; along with the colored light
that fell across our tables, the sheen
of the river running off in the dark.
The scent of sex in synthetic fabric.

Sometimes just a tress of hair can release
desire, and so can a single scent.
They can leave a life in shards.
This is the secret of charms and talismans,
not found in any lore. They do hold fate,
defining both the believer and his belief;
only the laughter that left those embankments
along the riverwalk can define anything more.

Double Entry

A lute strums beyond the window,
florins gleam on the fresh, white cloth:
the ledger can contrive the polis;
empty hands can always grasp death.
Across vistas workers die,
across time the campesinos are gleaned
like wheat.

In Spain, in Greece, in Guatemala,
in Chile and El Salvador,
his wit unleashed a bloodlust.
Such a simple, civilized gesture, such a profound
and clever invention: the coins gleam like drops
of golden blood.

When I Enter the Kingdom

Summer burns inside us,
its reflection shines, even if unseen, and out does
the fire of clouds and the poison of indignation.
    But we never choose to understand it.
It was sent to us as a consolation, while better gifts
perished among the blazing of planets, the sighting
of stars, the solstice that divides sight from light.

    Was it as if the poison of drugs
had made us stronger, had given the season just to us?
Proteus rising, Venus rising, Ganja scent
    rising in the night air.
When I and I enter the kingdom our eyes will burn
    like glass... when grass and grass
begin their blazing, a new kingdom will enter itself.
Schemes of averages retreat... the cement is soaked
with summer heat and ragged Venus returns from class,
her shoulders bronze above her bandaid halter, breasts
bulging, free of bra... armpit hair, the scent
of a woman's body.

    We all looked toward heaven
and let go imprudent cries, yes, bliss can grow
in torment... Austin was a magic city for years and years,
such scenes performed like ritual... Hero and Leander,
Venus and Anchises, hectic couples set the stakes
in heat, whole chains of empires and beings fade,

through them grief and joy mingled to wilt,
as they learned the yin and yang of the plains,
the gray-white Texas eternity.
The woods were dotted with the quick flickering of eyes,
surrounding the city of bright cafes.
Conversation surged and completed its quickening,
     Venus floated into town to entrapment,
suckered into all-night balls with gypsy women,
     Hero turned to size-up Anchises.

     But if anything maintains limits,
it's joy; only so much sunlight, so many dungarees,
round thighs, cool backyard evenings that go tumbling
to entwinements of hair and shapely torso.
The kingdom floats toward the open skylight,
Venus & co. carried with it. Only the stars hold
     their mythology… the rest of us are left
          a little angry and dull.

Our Cities Vanish

II

Zapotec

Hobos Near Tacoma

Bridge above the gorge,
lights of tightwadded Tacoma.

A chaff blown state,
sunlight yellow, wheat field yellow.

Everything gritty is also smooth:
riverbank, bed soil, rescue mission grit.

Like polished stone or sanded wood,
the view from any part of town
takes in the polish of lyrical land.

The bridge spans the gorge;
the trail leads to the bank like perdition.

Fifteen campfires pinpoint the bank;
even the stars lack shelter in Tacoma.

After Reading Boehme

This bridge, this water streaked with light,
images of decay descend into the depths,
    the water holds its beauty
the way you are held by life, the way embers
of being shine out in the evening.
    Gulls circle the lake, the glinting light;
are their cries any more real than what I
    would cry?
Words mean so little against loneliness, yet
we search for words, as if they alone
could counteract life.

Border Town

The Rio Grande flows like a hat band
under the international bridge.
When I went over, there was a small blue cross
wrapped in red and white wreaths
stuck in the sand below, fifty yards from
the railing, completely overlooked.
I stood and wondered who it could have been for.

Across the river adobe blazes white in the sun.
Dope smugglers buy drink for their unemployed
friends, liquor flows like a scalding sacrament,
as precious as the girls
who step from white afternoons offering themselves
for a handful of pesos... their brothers sell
shoes or Yankee newspapers.
The rubble moulds, shining in the sun, the fabric
of poverty laughing in the world's face.

Your Eyes Full of Weekends

After de Chapultepec, the Zona Rosa.
Red neon, red velvet, chances uncrumpled and hung
    like trappings for the tourists.
I could see you looking over my shoulder, your eyes
flashing in the half-dark window; your eyes
    full of weekends and late hours.
Walking brick streets, everything made of glass
or shiny metal reflected the train ride north,
    tracks converging,
thud-thudding into a continent crumpled to
a quarter its true size.
Town emerging ghost-like from the desert,
disappearing like the shifting faces. But your face
shone above it all, barely visible but shining,
    whispering something I could not understand.

Archives

I

In the summer
the elders frequent
the archives.
The musty smell
of old books
mingles
with their sense of repose.

The maidens and the wheat,
the sun
on their tiny feet,
your hand
upon
a slender waist.

II

The feet
are marching
as waves crash.
The feet
are marching
as waves crash.
The feet

are marching
as the sea of fists clench.
The answer
is not
in the archives.
The mouths
are marching,
the mouths
are marching,
and the minds are tossing slogans
while the Elders
dream
of rivers,
and lakes,
and ladies
in flowing gowns.
Walls are crumbling,
the horses bolt
and run
like a river.
The night is well lit,
the moon's teeth
are frantic;
but
the answer is not
in the archives.

III

The hour is like
a clock
wound too tight,
more like a fat balloon
when a child
won't stop blowing;
small faggots are abundant
and leak,
and the humble lintel.
The world
mutters
its sad stupidities
while the maiden
with the slender waist
advances.
Her lips fondle
the words
you will never hear;
"the answer is not in the archives."

Puntarenas

Things were much brighter when I was young.
We went to Costa Rica; at Puntarenas
it seemed like the waves lapped the beach
in blue flames.
The sun rose in a poppy-colored streak;
you could see a faint glow in the sea foam
at night.

But life is alike everywhere.
Life flattens like a wave breaking
across the shore.
We can see the tide's direction
only afterward, when the sea and coastline
become contingencies; the ocean will drone
until the shore is lapped back to water.
It is not the true color or shape of things
we understand best, but their repeated ebb.

Gnostic

Foot steps plot empty streets,
the city is a cinder in creation's fire.
Its glare breeds illness and unbalanced
notions.

St. Peter drew a bubble burst
by a saint with a bulging eye.
Walls of stone and the pagan priestess
prepare the leg of hollow-eyed
    beggars.
Still the vision lay beyond his raptured
senses,
    and no sight returned
as Hosanna rose with fragrant incense;
    the world lay ready for his fiery word.
From the mountains came rejoicing,
    and from valleys
came pot-ash and olive bearing doves.

He droned against it,
    against the fire and clouds of indignation
that crushed rebellion to its core.

We drove the camels, chest high in swirling dust,
    laying waste to the snares and tares of hell.
Then a holy terror seized us, and the world
    was woven into a tapestry of dust.

Artifacts

Wind blows grain across the ground,
the hills make the sun a legend, kingdoms were seen
falling from up there, some kingdoms rose,
the sun's glare, took them into the land…
bitter grain, brewed to distraction, snake coiled
in the shaman's leaf, the sun drew evening into
itself and made it part of the land,
only the mother could raise her hand to it all
and proclaim a course running apart from light.

We walked this far in silence. We felt her eyes
glaring behind meshes of leaf, her breasts
offered, hair woven out of flax. Nine spawns
clawed from the caves of this region, hundreds
more built on fields that absorbed their work;
our harvest slices to debris the sun chose not
to cancel, all discarded, no longer part of its
region: a crude child's rattle, a stone-made
screw-top jar.

The Ex-Missionary Learns Mexico

After the rain we came into the low
country, the hills unrolled beneath us,
pitted with arroyos; green aloe vera plants,
concealed basins where water stood,
hidden from high ground like secret lakes.
We climbed from our horses and looked into
a pond, our faces shining against sky
and cloud.

There is nothing holy about hidden things;
chance has its own way of breaking monotony
as one mile slinks
into the dust of another, but in this place
(out of millions all over the desert)
what seemed so dry from the trail's rim lay
entangled with fertility, floating
in a bath of sky.

For years I had learned the desert from train
windows, its beauty no more than swirling dust,
but when our faces rippled over brown roots,
dark as cinnabar, shooting into leafy green…
the vistas around us rose in vapor and begged
for a drink, in the distance a vulture called,
and hundreds of zacadas; the hills rose
above us like domes.

The Shaman Considers His Craft

Did I say footprints?
Did I say each puddle reflects a world?
I used to see distinction in things
other people instinctively ignore.
The bird in the bush could sing his door wide,
and with windows
there to open
the wealth of those deeper places could catch
the thrush's warble and glitter white fire.

But then I got to naming things,
and relating one thing to another.
The tracks for instance, no longer just a trail
to follow, an extension of some place where
the mystery of places might echo a brittle
birth.
I had to know that beauty—decode it,
like a song. The thrush's song, the broken tracks,
the little brown splotch that is the bird upon
its branch, it had to be a destiny, a metaphysic
or sympathy breaking down haunted tomes…
levels of justice and fate.

I had to know what made the haunted real,
to know how these doors open, one into another
so that bird sails freely

and his fire pierces through the bush, the puddles
that are slick as sliding glass,
and know much more than being carried
by a song (his song from his landscape)
into a scape not mine and not his.
And at that point, that beauty that became
so brittle as I went downward
(through the landscape his beauty built
into the scape not mine and not his)
I missed the whole haunted meaning of fire
and magic both.
And I was left there, as if I stood before
a maze of bushes all grown with doors.

In a Village at Night

The fountain in the square flows
serenely over stone; its sound has followed me
    through the market
and along back streets. I have passed old men
huddled in doorways, and younger men drinking,
groups of villagers singing away late hours.
The altar in the church is silent,
so I have said your name to the pigeons, and to
the night, hearing your name in the fountain,
it murmurs you over hills and deep skies.

Of course the night never cares who we love,
she whispers you through the fountain
because she knows my dreams are too impervious,
and though the day reflects places I could
have held you, plants your image among stoneworks,
groups of old women, the bodies of thin, dark girls,
it is the Mexican night that will not reveal
its secrets. Does the fountain speak your voice
or carry it through the night? Speak more
softly, though you are a thousand miles away.

Beauty in the Brain

The soul hovers beyond the trees,
beyond the clouds, beyond the stars.
I'm an empty shell that buys things,
and yet it's in me.

Does it flutter beyond the broken columns
and green glades, whispering their beauty
into my brain?
Perhaps they're in me too.

The soul is a ball of light that flutters
beyond. It's a jagged ball,
with edges that cut.
It's a mouth that feeds upon itself.

Yet the soul is also the glades
and hills and broken columns.
It's the part of me that knows
and doesn't know.
The soul is bigger than the self
that seeks it.

Monte Albán

Another night falls upon Oaxaca:
the trees around the Zócalo sprout blossoms
as purple as blood beneath the skin.
    This is the center of the town's life;
green palms bathed in blue light,
    shadows full of couples and cafes full
of bright laughter. This hardly seems like
    the birth place of Juárez, but his
statue stands on a hill near the edge of town
    smiling on the freedom he helped
        his people win.

But they have not all won the same freedom.
Just beyond the square the streets break up
    into rows of markets,
they break into pot holes and fill with mud,
    the sun bakes grime into old walls,
herds of people move urgently through dark stalls
    packed full of fish and fresh bread. Swarmed by
flies, stall racks hold hand woven fabrics,
    thick fabrics covered with bright prints.
The streets are full of thieves, braggarts,
    Gente sin Pensamiento.

Older men go north of the Zócalo to drink;
    squatting in small groups
    outside shabby bars, they sing

very old songs and talk about their women.
   This side of freedom saddens Juarez;
but the older guardians up in the hills,
   the old Zapotec spirits who
         watch over Monte Albán,
they know one generation cultivates another
   in the clarity of wind...
the old spirits are as aloof as the stones
   where they sit reigning over the region.
You have to know them to see their passion,
   you have to know them through the place.
You have to walk through the wind temple
      letting the narrow passages
take you up to the stone-carved heaven,
the heaven laid out by stars... or twirl
   into the rock with the geometric dancer,
twirl into regions that send the wind across
   fields gorged out in the sides of steep
peaks. All this before you know Benito
   must have stirred something
         in his Elders.

   After you arise with the wind,
you grow chilled with fear... the carvings
   at Monte Albán are stained with blood
the rain won't wash out. After last light bathes
   this land in its only true gold,
night winds impart the stench, reveal the King-

seer as little more than exalted slave.
   Kingdoms sprung from innocent blood
pass their lineage wearily to those
   who long for justice. Benito
must have made them wonder. But then,
   (just as you have to know the town
below to see past the beauty of the Zócalo),
you have to know these ruins to hear
   the old kings grumble.

   The Spanish once thought the old gods
lived in a higher heaven, until they rebelled
   against their maker.
That primordial war threw them from windless
   parts of heaven to their walls and altars;
they washed the blood of one victim
   with the blood of thousands.
   What the conquistador couldn't see
was the wheel of myth and conquest, perhaps
it was the memory of their special place,
   of laughter leaping bright as love,
that inspired the works at Monte Albán.

A Philosopher is Born in the Tropics

Alone again, the ex-missionary
regards his wine glass, the resort cafe
fills with clientele, he remains aloof,
inspired by the light's reflection on his glass.

Below the veranda, shouts recall confusions,
love never conquered, a girl's laughter,
gibes thrown too quickly; objects
and events open the soul like a blossom.

He steeps in his own lush thought—
puffs of color fed by moss, by the death
and rebirth of the moon and sun,
nourished but steeping to a wilted lump.

The bond between love and beauty double:
droning waves, speculations, the wheel
that takes the sun and stars around... love traces
it among the skies; God drawn by dots.

But to trace their beauty out in jungle
is to leave the blossom halted, half formed.
Beauty of heaven or a woman's body, either side
of love is the patch of light floating in wine.

Fire Shadow

"The fire is blessed, so is the shadow of fire,
we behold the vision of one in the other."
These were the words Heraclitus dreamed when youth
stained his bed with tears.

Old age gave him wisdom: "if the shadow of fire
is blessed, the image of fire is holy, for without
the image of fire we would burn; *this* is the fire
that kindles all elements."
But the nearness of death drove him mad:
In stupidity some have said, "the sun is the center
of everything, but even the mouth of a worm
is greater than the sun, for we work by the sun's grace,
but the worm takes away our toil!"

To Eileen in a Dream

    Obsessed with the thoughts
of solitary men, voices calling in wind.
    I came to wear your rivers, your
        silver nights.

I came to regale you in an Angel's mask, offering
    beauties too great to bear.
I saw you looking, sitting among rocks and weeds,
and when I leaned into your face, saw the reflection
of a house within your eyes.

III

Detail its Hidden

Returning From the South

Wonder World lies across
the Rio Grande.
The neon Camel range, the drag racer pit,
this country is nothing more than a big
amusement park.
Goat ropers in floppy cowboy hats,
dragster pilots in plastic suits,
truckstops overflowing with beefy looking people;
flaccid skin, puffy eyes, bright wardrobe.
The Motel south of Austin
calls itself Hacienda South; the only Spanish
is the maids who work silently and smile too much.

The lady by the pool is an English
professor. She can't see her field is dying.
She likes office supplies and computer printouts.
Her skin is puffy and pale; it won't tan
no matter how long she lies in the sun.
She lies on her stomach, legs poised in the air
like a bathing beauty,
though the race driver staying across the courtyard
always looks the other way when he walks around
the pool.

Apollo Runs a Theater in Harlem
Nike Makes Running Shoes

Even the moon looks pockmarked.
Subduing my human; knowing where to look.
I can see it side-lit, a chunk
   of old rock.
I can see it fall through orbit
over barren parking lots
where the oblong, blockhouse offices
reflect a wasted white or sickly
   silver.

Everything in this city glows or shines
or burns out. I never knew nature had
so many ugly hues. It tinges the contours
of light, so each sight reflects the struggle
to keep the moon the moon,
the farms free of city, to keep the city
from stealing light.

Everything we make is ugly *and* radiant,
as my cigarette pack says: "art is what
you blend."

Images from a Relationship

I

We walk around holding hands,
but nothing grows inside her, nothing pounds,
nothing sprouts wings;
we sit in bars holding hands, something drones
deep inside her—a counterpoint
to the clink of half-filled glasses.
Hand in hand we lie in sleep.
Even when we dream we dread my roommate's
return.

II

Leafy shadows on the walls of my room,
delicate shapes—weary desire.
Her voice calls me in sleep, calls
all the way from Austin.
A ghost walks through my skull, my
image-laden skull.

City lights beckon in the river,
we boast and drink a lot, days pass
in a delicate way—they drag us north
to grow stiff again in Dallas.

III

If someone tills the earth,
someone has to be bound to it.
I see her survey the sky, perhaps her fingers
can feel the grass and learn to love its touch.
Perhaps the passion of the earth will make her
love only phony men. Dig in the ground but can't find
the right shaped stone.

Her Voice Along the Phonewire

    I said:
"I wish I could reach out and touch you."
—"And I wish I could reach out and touch you."
The phone sent our conceits across the land
we had traveled,
each of us now living at opposite points.

    A ghost had been singing,
the stars seemed more ancient, women cooled
their brows with ice brought down from mountains
by men in black suits… it was for those same men
the women burned.
A sprig of clover on a dark glass pane,
a whisper, something about feverish night.
Giants cuddled among bull rushes
in sudden celebration, also in despair.

The World Revolves Around You

The sun broke through a cloudy morning.
It fell through disappearing blue and burst
    like a flower pot.
It splattered and ran down cliffs and along
the sloping beach.
It seeped over the sand, oozed into the sea
and covered the fine strands of coral.

    But of course it rose again.
It rose, pierced the maiden's head of cloud,
    shining
where we walked in the black sand
(we called it black—really ash gray).
Our eyes swept the beach, the sand swept back,
as if a crew of workmen had gazed all night.

The sun went pale again, a gull soared
through a translucent sky.
I thought your eyes were silver, or they were blue.
An inner sequence keeps time with the waves,
it changes like the waves change with light; you hang
like an ornament in these surroundings. Eyes
blue or silver, your voice could be a windchime
    or a gull calling…
but you yourself won't change, though I might
even re-create the world.

Priggish Fred Finds His Misery

The thing performs; he obliges like the river.
    He watches the barges, listens to
the traffic, the chugging of old coal barges.
The river has carved the bank, defined the town,
now it is the town's to formulate, just as he
    belongs to the thing that plays him.
Ithaca rises among the Alps, Doric columns
in the Black Forest, he drums dithyrambs
below Helen's palace.
He would have her Helen, have her Gretchen,
but he can't make the Rhineland sprout olives.

His wife's voice gleams across bright trestles,
rings through the court, stirring the bells
of Weimar, she talks funny, reeks cheap perfume:
"vat little slut has ousted Lotte. She has seen
the duke and vood the whizard of Weimar."

Something plays him like a drum.
The Neo-classical Shaman; Faust with a PhD.
But his wife prepares the tribal pit.
First Gretchen, then Helen, then column of smoke.
They watch the river, an infinity away from
Frankfort.
    She exhales a puff of smoke,
he runs a knife across her throat.

Madonnas and Modernity

Desire can grow for a single woman,
until she reflects an entire race.
Isaac's love for Rebecca was multiplied
by millions;
whoever carved the St. Demetra of Eleusis
thought he knew a woman who could contain
the cosmos;
today we multiply evenings by the sum
of a city's lights.

Our vigils are easily broken... a gaze
on the sunlit sidewalk, or a quick glance on
the sidewalk at night
(hair draping bare shoulders, brighter, more
alluring than yellow silk) and the breeze
can singe like the burning bush.
If her vigor mocks all modesty, a glance will
gain more than many looks, each look
multiplies into a life of lost chances.

Ardor burns the glazed muse into modernity,
but the dome of the church will not open
or crack, those realms where images reign always
descend, gazing on the rough-hewn wood will not
carry us far once we leave the vestry;

and I hope against feeble reality for a Madonna
of desire, but if you hope your gaze is rewarded
by her grace, then a glance is all you get.

Suburban Prophet

Wind blows across distant fields…
murmurs… cool in the evenings…
   Winds blow across distant fields,
the shade tree sways from the window seat.

All day it's been like meditation,
the evening breeze… cross-legged when city lights
come in the distance. In the street, the world's
destiny scrawled by a child's hand
   upon the pavement.
And so Tim the adman rises in the night
to slaughter his wife.
   Tim sets the clock that is set for eternity.
Outside Jacob's ladder descends on the front lawn,
glowing brighter than Broadway.
Music of Angels rings out beyond this paper,
His life has lead up to this vision:

   a double edged axe,
a black robed figure with the face of Tim's
alarm clock, figures dancing in each other's arms
   (quietly, beyond the fringe of woods)…

   Tim, the adman, rises to murder his wife,
or her cat, or perhaps a random variable… he ascends
the ladder into a neon bliss.

Calibrations in the Art of Character

The boy inside us all
plays hard to get; can anyone else know why?
I'm glued inside this shell, but animated,
real enough to fit inside a suitcase,
but tested and defined by the dead.
Entranced by rain, unable to call certain beauties
to perform, though even the grey rain is real.

The woman he wants is sick of pity;
she sits in a room of multi-colored glass,
death coiled inside her.
Blue trees and green lift her hands to the sky,
she prays like a schoolgirl, though sick
of the grey rain she feels the sun is bitter:
save us from the bitter sun, but dry us
in the cold grey rain.

There is a nail in her heart,
knowing she believes for the blue and green trees,
knowing the boy inside us all put on a pose.
He would become a living prayer of sorts,
made great by the eminence of death,
real enough to coil inside himself.

Woman of Cloth

Your husband dined with a woman of cloth
and sang bravely beneath his sea...
You carried him at that point, wrapt nomenclature,
because he had not heart to carry.
An afterthought struck when a sword burned my brain;
I transferred your beauty to the sea cliffs.

So I tilled his fields with a twisted hoe,
tilled them until I could brandish that blade
and hack open miles of boxes.
And each box contained little husbands, dolls,
puppets, and a wooden mask; each haunting me,
each chattering, finally they sang in unison:
"Her heart is a dead cause, her voice is soft,
but it's swollen, therefore her beauty
is just a dent in time."

It was also like grief.
I never admitted it until things grew ragged,
until I hung the fields with paper dolls,
begging for that sword to slash them.
So, as he weaves his wound this loom languishes,
he longs to sow up the nomenclatures.
But I have you, I see you in a garden of melons,
no longer cloth, though entangled by silver vines.

Craving the Moon-Like Aspirin

The night called it all too thin;
it wore a sombrero hat, it poured gray coffee.
It came boating on glasses and tableware.
It tingtinged light through crystal.
It poured a simple water, lost in edges of light,
garnish for the eye before the eye
is stung with smoke.
It made a little incense.

It smelled like sex and crumpled flowers.
Then it was full of women.
Women that went gray like its rotten coffee.
Women caught in my jagged teeth.
Women embossed with light around the edges.
Thin fingers, bone clothed by wrinkles
but nimble like the tingtinging silver,
eyes brighter than smoke… the affair stings
like smoke but won't burn.

Then taxi rides.
The streets flat or winding.
The streets put out for the evening.
The streets put out but hung
with gobs of yellow light.
Pinpoints like the women. Even more:
the bright black hair, then the breasts
and thighs go firm.

The shear, sliding intoxicant, young flesh,
all accouterments, beauty like a standard
transmission.

Now the night furnished its code.
It spoke of things burning.
Everything edged in light.
Everything grew arid or alluring, and the moon
broke out a thousand epithets. I climbed them
like a set of stairs,
but they brought no more women.
Pipes rusted, Pan won't sing.
Leaves waving neither hello nor goodbye.
But they too are edged in light:
subtle, sickly, all too sweet, coffee cup
with three packets.

Arguing the Past Away

We broke up. We broke up again.
I wasn't finished, I argued the past away.
For the rest of my youth I waited
for her, only her memory came.
Then it came; first in my mind
it came as if it were her—walking out
of the haze in the distance, it was late
evening—then I saw her from my window,
just as she had looked in my mind's eye.

And with her were the evenings, all
the ambitions and endless fantasy.
     She walked onto the patio, laughed
insanely, and brought the entire past
          to confrontation.
We drove the restless streets we drove
          when we were young.
We argued and parted, reconciled and
parted again, over all the same
          issues.

Then reality brought this thing to a
merciful end.
          There in the patio's half light.
with only a dozen stars to oversee
this profound event. I burned the last
          of her letters.

I said an obligatory prayer (but rapidly, without thinking) and parted with youth forever.

Waking was a Reawakening

Waking was a reawakening
    after the diction of sleep
connected us to the dreamers our actions
portray.

    That was when I really knew you,
when it was dark and the rain lent us a kind
of protection, falling on the faithless dead.
It was neither waking nor sleeping; it was
something that could hide us from the pain
engendered by a perfect pleasure.

    "Phonewires bind the earth," you said,
speaking from another part of that region of
somnambulods, "out of all the flirtations
that ended in anger, out of all the glasses
Mozart drinks, nothing is immune to our voices,
no one can hide from us."

    Then, by the essence of this hypnagogic logic
we found tiny people living between us,
a city spread across silk sheets. Adobe, thatch,
an entire city's patchwork waste with us
on either side.

Whitman's Ghost Takes a Tour of the City

The goddess sits in the axe handle park,
she would give more grain, but corn won't grow
in our streets.
The trees can lift their arms skyward,
but their hands and hair sprout flames.
     Eidólons time, Eidólons time,
when the old shade goes loafing (though evening
can't come any closer). Could he manage disembodiment
before now, the fire of the flower would still
be there by chance.

But you, knowing the richer reds
and deeper blues appear briefly at dusk
then withdraw into their own flame...
He goes out at evening, shirt long, baggy as a coat,
his white beard flows from the sack-like face,
the outstretched hat-brim,
he has made himself bewildered; where are the poets
chanting to the multitude? The headlong, vulgar, robust
freedoms of the crowd? Is there only you?
Bleating out this quick-flaring image? You chant
the gawk-shuffle, art-patter, and wonder how the plant
ever let you in. The inferno of the city blazes
around us; we detail its hidden lights.

The New World Order #1

The buildings have invaded fields,
the sun glances off archribbed mirrors.
White, sterile
chunks of slab with fake porticos.
Homes were scraped aside
for row upon row of random cars,

the sky
is pelted with lights
that slide from one horizon to the next,
the powdery sheet of stars
is blotted out.
None of this has given us our freedom,
though our freedom reclaimed these fields.

Corporations Buy and Sell

Corporations buy and sell,
kingdoms rise and fall,
goods surge like rivers of traffic,
the poor huddle in their peeling apartments;
the opposition: slender types in black,
with their MAs in creative writing,
chattering lists of platitudes
to a crowd that applauds
everything it hears.

Rivers boil away, woodlands wither,
species die out,
fighters fight, ranters rant,
everyone makes their living from
a dieing planet.

Sometimes I go out to look at the moon,
radiant white or chili pepper red,
lost in the clutter of lights.
Does it remember the things we have given up?
The moon just smiles and says nothing.

The Thing You Will Miss Most

Against the whirl of night life
    you hold your heart
    like some fragile glass thing
that hums approval or hatred.
We should lament the loss of higher things.
    But when our democracy is gone,
this will be the thing you miss most.

Our Cities will Vanish

the way they were built,
in flurries of greed and seduction.
Dallas for instance,
was founded by Appalachian
Pariahs,
lean men with gaunt faces
and a burning in their eyes.
Now another Dallas has sprung up
where they built,
a Mecca for the mercenaries
wrapped in steel glitter,
wrapped in gold glitter, burning as brightly
as their lust.
Practicality is their monument
to their fathers.
Practicality,
the faith of Pariahs:
the gleam of a bauble pawed by cats.
When pressed
they will admit truth is beautiful.
Nature
for instance,
is even more beautiful
when its mysteries are revealed, and so
they still admire the moon,

praise it,
for remaining such a worthy objective
for their calculations
of trajectory,
they admire Einstein, who "thought up some good physics,"
that will allow them to build other Dallases
on distant planets.
Eternity is Profound.
And yet,
the only eternity they believe in
is the eternal distance between classes,
between races,
between failure and success.

Our cities will vanish
the way they were built,
and return even more mysteriously.

References

ACHILLES AND ANDROMACHE - In Greek mythology, Andromache was the wife of Hector. During the Trojan War, Achilles killed Hector and Achilles' son Neoptolemus (originally Pyrrhus) took Andromache as concubine.

AGAMEMNON'S BOAST - According to Homer, Agamemnon was ready to launch his fleet to attack Troy. They could not sail because Artemis (the goddess of hunting) has stilled the wind. She had been offended when Agamemnon had boasted after killing a stag that not even she could not have done it better. To return the wind, the goddess demanded the sacrifice of Agamemnon's daughter, Iphigenia.

APOLLO AND DAPHNE - From Greek mythology. After Apollo chided Eros for playing with a bow and arrows, the young god shot the nymph Daphne with a lead arrow (that made her hate Apollo) and Apollo with the gold one (that made him love Daphne). Daphne fled Apollo and was escaping until Eros intervened. Daphne called upon her father to save her by having the earth swallow her or changing her into something else. Her father turned her into the bay laurel tree.

ARROYO - The vertical walled deep creek beds common throughout the United States Southwest. The word is also the literal Spanish word for a brook.

ARYANS - An older synonym for Indo-European that comes from the term 'arya' in ancient Hindu and Zoroastrian texts. For the Nazis, Aryans were a "master race" whose civilization dominated the world from Atlantis on until "inferior" races mixed with the Aryans after the destruction of Atlantis.

BEEHIVE (hairdo) - One style of elaborate lacquered "big hair" popular in the 1960's that resembles a beehive. By the 1970's, it had become associated (perhaps thanks to TV) with stereotypical diner waitresses. It is also known as a B-52 (because of the resemblance to the nose of the B-52 "Stratofortress" bomber) and is regarded as symbol of 1960's kitsch.

BELLS OF WEIMAR - The centenary of Schiller's death was marked by the ringing of church bells throughout Germany. The scene in Weimar is described in German Memories by Sidney Whitman

BHAGAVAD GĪTĀ (Between 500 and 200 BCE) - A sacred scripture considered authoritative in most Hindu traditions that has widespread influence in the west in music, art, business and even physics. J. Robert Oppenheimer, Director of the Manhattan Project, upon witnessing the world's first nuclear test in 1945, quoted it: "Now I am become Death, the destroyer of worlds" (ch 11, vs 32).

BOEHME, JACOB (1575 - 1624) - German Christian mystic and theologian; held similar belief to the Holy Cabala (alternately Kabbala or Qabala) God is immanent within his creation like embers of fire within a smoldering log. Also known as Jakob Bohme.

CAMPESINOS - This term probably entered usage in the United States as a name for Mexican farm workers who participated in the Bracero Program during World War II in the United States. Since at least the 1930's in Spain and the Americas, the term has meant groups of workers and at times, workers unions and politically active worker groups.

CROSSVINE (Bignonia capreolata) - A flowering semi-evergreen vine, also known as quatervine, that is native to 17 U.S. States.

DE CHAPULTEPEC - Chapultepec Castle (Castillo de Chapultepec in Spanish) is located on top of Chapultepec Hill in the middle of Chapultepec Park in Mexico City at 7,628 ft. above sea level. The building is currently the Mexican National Museum of History but, since it was built in the 18th century, has served many roles, including as the palace of Emperor Maximilian I of Mexico and his wife Empress Carlota.

St. Demetra of Eleusis - The Goddess Demeter was unofficially canonized by the people in the region of her ancient city.

Dithyramb - originally an ancient Greek hymn sung to the god Dionysus. Although rare, wildly enthusiastic speech or writing is occasionally described as dithyrambic.

Clint Eastwood - Award winning actor, director and producer known for his iconic macho characters in movies such as the Spaghetti Westerns of Sergio Leone and the Dirty Harry films, credited as creating the loose-cannon cop genre.

Eidólons - Dictionaries variously defined Eidólon as (1) a phantom or apparition, (2) An image of an ideal. Eidólons is the title of a poem by Walt Whitman that appears in Leaves of Grass. Some believe that it means "Of the multitude" in that context.

Gente Sin Penetermas (Colloquial slang) - Those who have no thoughts; bullies.

Geometrical Dance - Originated in the Renaissance emphasized the number of dancers and the elaborate patterns traced on the dancing floor, as much as the gestures and shapes of the individuals' performing. It was modeled on the cosmic dance as described by Plato and his successors.

Gretchen - Woman seduced by Faust in Goethe's Faust with tragic consequences for the child she has with Faust and for herself.

HELEN AND PARIS - Helen was married to Menelaus, King of Sparta. Depending on the source, Paris either seduced or kidnapped her and returned to Troy. When Menelaus discovered she was gone, he called on Helen's suitors and so began the Trojan War.

HERACLITUS (c. 500BCE) of Ephesus - The first Western philosopher to look beyond physical theory to metaphysical foundations and their moral application. He said that the Logos —everlasting Word— is the foundation of the universe, that change (not things or substances) is central to the universe, and that the law of nature manifests as human moral law.

HERO AND LEANDER - In Greek Mythology, the young man Leander fell in love with Hero, a priestess of Aphrodite. Every night, he swam across the Hellespont straight to be with her and after a time, Hero succumbed to his gentle words. This situation lasted through the summer until one stormy winter night. The wind blew out Hero's light and Leander lost his way. He was drowned and Hero was grief-stricken and threw herself from the tower and died.

HOSHANA/HOSANNA - Transliterations of Biblical Hebrew and Greek words that are both a cry for salvation and a declaration of praise. Hoshana is used during Sukkot, a Judaic festival associated with securing rain for the following year. Hosanna was shouted in adoration and praise to recognize the Messiahship of Jesus as he entered Jerusalem shortly before his crucifixion (Matthew, Mark and John).

ILIOS - Another name for the legendary city of Troy: the city and country of the Trojans. The name is echoed in Illium, the name of a city founded on the traditional site of Troy, during the reign of Roman Emperor Augustus.

INDO-EUROPEAN - (now referred to by many scholars as Proto-Indo-European) is the name for a culture that was the language (and presumably cultural) basis for all Mythological-age cultures in both Europe and India. Hitler gave them credit for fathering the Aryan race.

ISAAC'S LOVE FOR REBECCA - According to Genesis, After Sarah died, Abraham sets out to find a wife for his 37 year old son Isaac. He sends a servant, Eliezer, to Abraham's home to select a bride. Eliezer prayed "Let it be the maiden to whom I shall say, 'Please tip over your jug so I may drink,' and who replies, 'Drink, and I will even water your camels,' her will You have designated for Your servant, for Isaac". A young girl, Rebecca, immediately came out and offered to draw water for him and to water his camels.

JACOB'S LADDER – *And he dreamed that there was a ladder set up on the earth and the top of it reached to heaven; and the angels of God were ascending and descending on it!* (Genesis 28:12, Amplified Bible). The use of Jacob's Ladder in the poem "Suburban Prophet" is interesting in light of two additional points. First, Alan Landsburg and Leonard Nemoy (*In Search Of Extraterrestrials,* Bantam Books, 1976) discussed the idea that this passage refers to extraterrestrial visitors. Second, the 1997 suicides by members of the Heaven's Gate cult, were motivated in part by the desire to ascend to a UFO riding the tail of the comet Hale-Bopp.

BENITO JUÁREZ – was a five-time President of Mexico. He is often regarded as Mexico's greatest leader for his role in resisting and overthrowing the French occupation of Mexico and modernizing the country. He was the first full-blooded indigenous national to lead a Western Hemisphere country in over 300 years.

KALIDASA (5th century CE) - Indian Poet who used the cloud messenger as his allegory of the divine aspect of Romantic Love.

MAGUEY - An Agave (as opposed to a cactus) used to produce Pulque (the predecessor of Mescal and Tequila). Pulque had a privileged place in mythology, religion and economics of Mesoamerica. Traditionally, drinkers in pulquerías slop a small amount of the drink from their glass on the floor as a sacrifice to Two Rabbit (one of many gods associated with Pulque).

MARCUSE - A German philosopher and sociologist. He was a member of the Frankfurt School known for his critiques of capitalist society.

MONTE ALBÁN (ca. 500 BCE - 500 CE) - A large archaeological site in the southern Mexican state of Oaxaca. The civic-ceremonial center of the site is situated atop an artificially-levelled ridge at about 6400 feet. The site is important both because it is one of the earliest known cities of Mesoamerica and the Zapotec sociopolitical and economic center for close to a thousand years.

OAXACA - A Mexican state located southwest of the Yucatan Peninsula on the Pacific coast. Historically, Oaxaca is the home of the Zapotec and Mixtec peoples. Currently it has more speakers of indigenous languages than any other Mexican state.

ODYSSEUS' BOW - In Homer's Odyssey, Odysseus (or Ulysses) takes ten years to return home after the Trojan War. When he returned, he learned that his wife Penelope had remained faithful. But, her suitors finally demanded that she choose a new husband. She told them that whoever could string Odysseus' bow and shoot an arrow through 12 axe-handles would marry her. But only Odysseus could string his bow.

PAN'S WIFE - In Greek Mythology, the God Pan had the upper body of a human and the hindquarters, legs and horns of a goat. In one story, the water-nymph Syrinx was trying to escape his advances. Her sisters changed her into a reed to hide her. Pan, still infatuated, cut down the reeds and cut them to form the pan flute he was known for. In another story, the nymph Echo scorned the love of every man. This angered Pan. His followers tore her to pieces and scattered her over the earth. In some version, they had a child: Iambe.

PERSHING (1960 - 1991) - Medium range surface-to-surface guided nuclear missiles named for General John J. Pershing. They were in the US Army inventory until the last was eliminated under the terms of the Treaty on Intermediate Range Nuclear Forces. The INF Treaty was notable because it was the first to eliminate an entire class of nuclear missiles.

PRIGGISH FRED: From Faust.

PROTEUS RISING - Proteus, in Greek mythology, was a sea god and one of several deities whom Homer calls the "Old Man of the Sea". Carl Jung defined Proteus as a personification of the unconscious, who, because of his gift of prophecy and shape-changing has much in common with the central but elusive figure of alchemy, Mercurius. The phrase "Proteus Rising" appears in an 1807 William Wordsworth sonnet:

> ...I'd rather be

A Pagan suckled in a creed outworn;
So might I, standing on this pleasant lea,
Have glimpses that would make me less forlorn;
Have sight of Proteus rising from the sea.

PUNTARENAS - The capital and largest city in Costa Rica's Puntarenas province. Located on the Pacific coast. The word means "sandy point".

QUETZALCÓATL - The Aztec sky and creator god who was often referred to as The Feathered Serpent. Quetzalcóatl was the patron god of the priesthood, learning and knowledge and associated with the planet Venus. The name comes from the words quetzal (brightly colored Mesoamerican bird) and coatl (serpent). The name was also taken on by various ancient leaders.

REAGAN'S DAUGHTER - Patti Davis (born Patricia Ann Reagan) has had many well-publicized conflicts with her parents and was called the black sheep of their children. She married her yoga instructor Paul Grilley in 1984. Patti Davis later reconciled with her parents, particularly as the family dealt with her Father's Alzheimer's disease.

ROBINSON JEFFERS (1887 - 1962) - An American poet known for his work about the central California coast and considered an icon of the environmental movement.

ROTCY BOY - An R.O.T.C. Candidate.

SYNAPSE - Specialized connections (containing a small gap) through which neurons signal each other.

TAURIANS (1st Millennium BCE - 300 AD) - Inhabitants of the mountainous regions of the Crimea that engaged in animal husbandry, agriculture and coastal fishing. They were technologically less advanced than their neighbors but managed to survive as a separate group until they were assimilated by the Alans, Goths and other invaders.

TIRESIAS (also transliterated as Teiresias) was a blind prophet of Thebes. According to some stories, the gods blinded him for revealing their secrets. Callimachus' poem "The Bathing of Pallas" says that Athena blinded him after he stumbled on her bathing naked. Tieresias mother Chariclo, a nymph of Athena, begged her to undo the curse.

Athena could not, but she cleaned his ears, giving him the gift of augury.

VENUS AND ANCHISES - In Roman mythology, Anchises was a mortal lover of the goddess Venus (Aphrodite in Greek mythology). In some version of the story, Aphrodite pretended to be a princess and seduced Anchises for nearly two weeks of lovemaking. Nine months later, Venus revealed that she was a goddess and presented him with the infant Aeneas.

WIZARD OF WEIMAR - Tchaikovsky's (only half-facetious) description of Franz Liszt, the creator of the piano recital.

ZACADA - Mexican term for type of locust commonly known as a Cicada in the southern U.S.

ZÓCALO - The main plaza or town square of many cities and towns in Mexico.

ZONA ROSA - A section of Colonia Juarez in Mexico City called the pink zone because of the pink tiles on the street. The area over time became a business, commercial, social and tourist center. In the 1960s, art galleries were created with the support of artist and intellectuals such as José Luis Cuevas and Guadalupe Amor. The cosmopolitan feature of the area attracted local and international visitors which encouraged the creation of hotels, jewellers, nightclubs, handicraft markets as well as the city's best restaurants and antique stores. Today, it is one of the city's most touristy areas, filled with hotels, dance clubs, restaurants, bars and live bands.

Ray Hinman returns the strength of history and culture to language. Unashamed of thought and uninhibited by poetic anti-intellectualism, Hinman speaks from a foun-

dation of traditions yet freshens his structures with the touch and sight of nature. Definitely modern, he unites civilization across time, refuses to surrender to the triviality of technology, though still hints that our era sticks out in defiance of human greatness. His rhythms flow with the love of language's music and, like the Whitman whose ghost tours his city, he finds in the urban tableau the clues to what we search for in clustering into cities.

He studied at the University of Texas at Arlington and the University of North Texas. He has traveled extensively in North and Central America.

Ray Hinman's work has been published in *Interstate, The Amoeba, Well Spring, Balcones, artsDFW* and *Negations: an Interdisciplinary Journal of Social Criticism.* He authored a previous collection of poems titled *A Rule of Three.*

Printed in the United States
143969LV00001B/8/P